W9-CLI-267

Essential Viewpoints

OBESITY &
FOOD POLICING

OBESITY &
FOOD POLICING

BY MARCIA AMIDON LUSTED

Content Consultant
Kathleen Keller, Ph.D., Research Associate
New York Obesity Research Center

ABDO
Publishing Company

CREDITS

Published by ABDO Publishing Company, 8000 West 78th Street, Edina, Minnesota 55439. Copyright © 2008 by Abdo Consulting Group, Inc. International copyrights reserved in all countries. No part of this book may be reproduced in any form without written permission from the publisher. The Essential Library™ is a trademark and logo of ABDO Publishing Company.

Printed in the United States.

Editor: Patricia Stockland
Copy Editor: Paula Lewis
Interior Design and Production: Nicole Brecke
Cover Design: Nicole Brecke

Library of Congress Cataloging-in-Publication Data
Lusted, Marcia Amidon.
  Obesity and food policing / Marcia Amidon Lusted.
      p. cm. — (Essential viewpoints)
  Includes bibliographical references and index.
  ISBN 978-1-60453-058-2
  1. Obesity—Social aspects—Juvenile literature. 2. Obesity—United States—Juvenile literature. I. Title.

  RA645.O23L87 2008
  362.196'398—dc22

                            2007031918

TABLE OF CONTENTS

Fast food is a mainstay of many Americans' lifestyles.

AN OBESITY EPIDEMIC?

n July of 2003, Surgeon General Richard Carmona, the highest-ranking medical official in the United States, appeared before the U.S. House of Representatives Committee on Education and the Workforce. He was there to testify about a crisis in American health:

> *As Surgeon General, I welcome this chance to talk with you about a health crisis affecting every state, every city, every community, and every school across our great nation. The crisis is obesity. It's the fastest-growing cause of disease and death in America.*[1]

Dr. Carmona's testimony was another warning voice in the growing concern throughout the medical community and in the media about the rising obesity rates in the United States. Soon called the obesity epidemic, Dr. Carmona's testimony paralleled statistics showing that obesity was increasing at an extremely rapid rate.

The Centers for Disease Control and Prevention (CDC) has estimated that among American adults ages 20 to 74, more than 60 percent are overweight. Of those people, almost 33 percent are considered obese. This is an increase of more than 15 percent from the 1970s. More children have become obese, too. As of 2007, reports showed that approximately 25 million children in the United States were considered overweight or obese.

The obesity problem is not limited to the United States. The World Health Organization (WHO) estimates that currently more than 1 billion adults are overweight throughout the world. This includes both modernized and developing countries. According to the WHO,

> *Increased consumption of more energy-dense, nutrient-poor foods with high levels of sugar and saturated fats, combined with reduced physical activity, have led to obesity rates that have risen three-fold or more since 1980. … The obesity epidemic is not restricted to industrialized societies; this increase is often faster in developing countries than in the developed world.* [2]

THE AMERICAN DIET AND LIFESTYLE

The United States is a land of fast-food restaurants, prepackaged snack foods, and a constant barrage of commercials and advertisements promoting delicious foods to eat. Most American families frequently eat in restaurants or bring home take-out food. According to Greg Critser in his book, *Fat Land: How Americans Became the Fattest People in the World*:

> *In 1970 what the USDA [United States Department of Agriculture] called the "food away from home" portion of the average American's food dollar was 25 percent; by*

1996 Americans were spending more than 40 percent of every food dollar on meals obtained away from home.[3]

Most take-out and fast foods contain more calories, fats, and sugars than meals prepared at home, which contributes to weight gain. Average portion sizes of food have increased while prices have decreased, leading to even more weight gain.

Children are especially vulnerable to advertising, particularly on television, that presents them with poor food choices in the guise of appealing snack foods and fast foods. The culture of food has also moved away from three traditional meals a day toward constant snacking or "grazing." A direct link has been shown between food advertisements and food intake. Most advertised or heavily marketed foods are high in fat and calories but low in vitamins and minerals. These food choices are often snacks or quick meals.

Come to America and Get Fat

Dr. Mita Sanghavi Goel, a researcher from the Northwestern University School of Medicine, has studied the rates of obesity among U.S. immigrants. Typically, these immigrants came from countries with lower obesity rates and were very rarely obese when they arrived in the United States. After one year in the United States, the rate of obesity among immigrants was at 8 percent. After 15 years, the rate was 20 percent. Immigrants may risk their health by adapting to the American way of eating.

Obesity is not just a product of food consumption. Americans, especially children and teens, also get less exercise. Sedentary activities such as watching television, playing video games, and using the computer have increased. More people now drive to work, school, and shopping centers instead of walking. All of these factors contribute to the obesity epidemic. Physical education classes in school have been cut back due to funding constraints and an increased emphasis on the academic basics. According to the WHO,

Large shifts towards less physically demanding work have been observed world-wide. Moves toward less physical activity are also found in the increasing use of automated transport, technology in the home, and more passive leisure pursuits.[4]

Which States Are the Fattest?

The CDC sponsored studies in 1991 and in 2001 to determine which of the 50 states had the highest percentage of obesity and what those percentages were. In 1991, only four states had an obesity rate of 15 percent or higher, and no state had a rate of over 20 percent. But just ten years later, only one state in the United States had an obesity rate below 15 percent (Colorado) and 29 states had rates above 20 percent. The fattest states in the country (as of the 2001 survey) were mostly located in the South. Mississippi topped the chart with a 25.9 percent obesity rate. West Virginia, Michigan, Kentucky, and Indiana followed at 24 percent. Texas, Alabama, and Louisiana had a 23 percent obesity rate.

In another survey conducted in 2005, the number of obese people continued to rise. Overall, the United States has overweight and obesity rates as high as 60 percent of the population. Among the 50 states, Hawaii has the lowest obesity rate at 15 percent.

Worldwide, people are eating more and moving less. One survey reports that more than 26 percent of adults are not involved in any leisure-time exercise.

Is Being Overweight a Problem?

American society and media regularly promote that the ideal person should be thin. Obesity, then, is often seen only in terms of appearance. But beyond feeling social pressures, people who are obese face other issues.

Health officials note that obesity leads to a variety of health problems, such as respiratory difficulties, sleep apnea, chronic bone and joint problems, skin problems, and infertility. These usually are not life threatening. But obesity also contributes to more serious problems, such as type 2 diabetes, high blood pressure, stroke, and coronary artery disease. Obesity is also linked to increased incidents of several types of cancer as well as osteoarthritis.

There has been a significant increase in the number of children who suffer from type 2 diabetes. Previously, this disease occurred mostly in adults. Before 1992, type 2 diabetes accounted for 2 to 4 percent of all childhood diabetes. By 1994, that percentage had increased to 16 percent.

The number of children suffering from this disease continues to rise.

Although the causes of obesity are numerous, the fast-food industry is increasingly blamed for the epidemic, particularly in children and teens. The issue of fast food's responsibility for the health of its customers is hotly debated. This leads some people to question if their weight is the fault of the fast-food industry and not their own eating habits.

Who is to blame: the fast-food industry or the person who chooses to eat fast food? Researcher Kathleen Keller, Ph.D., notes,

The causes of obesity are complex and related to both biology (genetics) and the environment. Therefore, it is difficult to put the blame on one institution for a disease [that] is truly multi-factorial.[5]

Child Abuse?

In 1996, 13-year-old Christina Corrigan died of heart failure as a result of her extreme obesity. Her mother, Marlene Corrigan, was convicted of child neglect for allowing her daughter to exist in filthy conditions and lay in her own waste among fast-food containers, unable to move because of her size. Marlene Corrigan's defense lawyer claimed that Christina's weight was due to a rare medical condition and not due to neglect on her mother's part. Marlene Corrigan avoided serving a six-year prison term and was sentenced to three years of probation and 240 hours of community service.

The Heart of the Controversy

U.S. Surgeon General Richard Carmona stated,

As we look to the future and where childhood obesity will be in 20 years ... it is every bit as threatening to us as is the terrorist threat we face today. It is the threat from within.[6]

Few people deny that obesity has become an epidemic in the United States and around the world. However, there is a big difference in viewpoints as to who is responsible.

If the United States is facing a health crisis because of its population's rising obesity levels, whose responsibility is it to deal with this issue? Should state and national governments increase legislation aimed at helping Americans eat properly and get more exercise? Or is it the individual's responsibility to decide what he or she eats—whether or not it results in weight gain? And if health care costs continue to rise because of obesity-related diseases, who should pay those higher costs? These are the fundamental issues at the heart of the obesity epidemic.

Should Americans be able to eat whatever they want, whenever they want? Should legislation restrict food choices in the interest of better health? Who has the ultimate say in controlling obesity: the person in the drive-through at a favorite fast-food restaurant or the legislators and health officials in Washington, D.C.? ⌐

The Heaviest Person in the World

One of the most obese people ever to be treated in a medical facility was Carol Yager of Michigan. She is estimated to have weighed more than 1,600 pounds (726 kg) at her heaviest. Despite losing nearly 500 pounds (227 kg) during a hospital stay, she regained that and more after being discharged. She died in 1994 at the age of 34 from water retention and kidney failure.

U.S. Surgeon General Richard H. Carmona

William Taft was president of the United States from 1909 to 1913, and he was chief justice from 1921 to 1930.

What Is Obesity?

What is obesity? What makes one person overweight while another person becomes obese? Why is obesity classified as a disease like cancer or heart disease?

Obesity in History

Obesity is not a new condition. Throughout history, obesity has existed and has even been encouraged in some cultures. Ancient Egyptians may have classified obesity as a disease. They usually mentioned it in connection with medical topics. But there are stories of an Egyptian pharaoh whose stomach was wider than the span of a man's height.

The Romans also mentioned several extremely overweight people, such as a senator who could only walk when two slaves carried his belly. A Greek king, Dionysus of Heracleia, was so heavy that he could hardly move. The Greeks also seemed to realize that obesity was a disease. The ancient Greek physician Hippocrates noted that overweight people were more likely to die suddenly than thin people.

In the nineteenth century, obesity was more socially acceptable than it is today. During that time, many people suffered from diseases such as tuberculosis, which made them appear gaunt and sick. Some felt that obese people looked healthier than those who were thin. Someone who was obese looked well fed and in good health. Heavy people were also viewed as prosperous and secure. Several U.S. presidents, such as Ulysses S. Grant, Chester

The Corn Syrup Revolution

Some researchers feel that one reason for the rising rates of obesity has to do with a shift in the way food is sweetened. In 1971, Japanese scientists found a way to create a sweetener from corn. High-fructose corn syrup is six times sweeter than sugar and can be produced inexpensively in the United States. The body breaks down corn syrup differently than regular sugars, possibly leading to storage of more fat. Water is the main ingredient in soft drinks, but high-fructose corn syrup is the second main ingredient in sodas that do not use low-calorie artificial sweeteners.

A. Arthur, and William H. Taft, were obese. They were elected partly because they appeared to be stable and trustworthy due to their weight.

As people have become more affluent and their lifestyles more sedentary, obesity has increased in the twentieth and twenty-first centuries. This is largely due to advanced machinery and technology that no longer requires people to perform heavy physical labor or walk long distances. As the population eats more processed food and fewer natural fruits, vegetables, and grains, changes in diet have led to increased incidences of obesity. In the twentieth century, at least 28 people appeared in the national and international media because they weighed in excess of 900 pounds (408 kg). Many were unable to leave their beds or walk because of their tremendous weight. Most died from medical complications related to obesity.

Defining Body Mass and Obesity

Doctors commonly use a measurement called body mass index, or BMI, to determine whether someone is overweight or obese. BMI is a number that measures body weight relative to height. To determine BMI, the person's weight in pounds is divided by their height in inches squared. That number is then multiplied by 703. Someone who is six feet tall and weighs 200 pounds has a BMI of 27.

Because children are still growing, BMIs are converted to percentile values in those under the age of 20. In children, a BMI above the 85th percentile is considered "at risk." Above the 95th percentile is considered overweight. For adults, the Centers for Disease Control and Prevention (CDC) defines a BMI below 18.5 as underweight. A BMI between 18.5 and 24.9 is normal; between 25 and 29.9 is overweight. A BMI over 30 is obese, and a BMI over 40 is morbidly obese.

An overweight person is someone who has an increased body weight relative to his or her height. A person who is overweight may not have excess body fat. They may simply be heavier than recommended for their height. An obese person has an excessive amount of body fat compared to lean body mass.

Weight in Pounds

Height	120	130	140	150	160	170	180	190	200	210	220	230
6'8"	13	14	15	17	18	19	20	21	22	23	24	25
6'6"	14	15	16	17	19	20	21	22	23	24	25	27
6'4"	15	16	17	18	20	21	22	23	24	26	27	28
6'2"	15	17	18	19	21	22	23	24	26	27	28	30
6'0"	16	18	19	20	22	23	24	26	27	28	30	31
5'10"	17	19	20	22	23	24	26	27	29	30	32	33
5'8"	18	20	21	23	24	26	27	29	30	32	34	35
5'6"	19	21	23	24	26	27	29	31	32	34	36	37
5'4"	21	22	24	26	28	29	31	33	34	36	38	40
5'2"	22	24	26	27	29	31	33	35	37	38	40	42
5'0"	23	25	27	29	31	33	35	37	39	41	43	45
4'10"	25	27	29	31	34	36	38	40	42	44	46	48
4'8"	27	29	31	34	36	38	40	43	45	47	49	52
4'6"	29	31	34	36	39	41	43	46	48	51	53	56

Height in Feet and Inches

☐ Healthy Weight   ☐ Overweight   ☐ Obese

Body mass is calculated using both height and weight.

Obesity is not just measured by weight. It is also determined by how much body fat the individual has. Obesity is broken down into three categories: mild, moderate, or morbid (also known as severe). These categories are based on factors such as ideal body weight, body fat distribution, age, degree of risk for medical problems, and amount of control over eating. A morbidly obese person is at least 100 pounds (45 kg) over their ideal body weight and is the most likely to develop severe health problems. Doctors also look at where the highest concentration of body fat is located. Excess fat in the abdomen is medically riskier than fat in the hips or legs. Patients with excess weight in the abdomen are usually classified as moderately or severely obese.

Doctors also use other systems of measurement, such as height and weight charts, and a patient's waist circumference, to determine obesity. A great deal of body fat concentrated in the abdomen puts the patient at a higher risk of diabetes, high blood pressure, and cardiovascular disease. Waist circumference measurement is usually combined with BMI to determine risk. If a man has a waist circumference of 40 inches (102 cm) or more, or a woman has a waist circumference of 35 inches (89 cm) or more, and a BMI higher than 25, they are considered to be at an increased risk for obesity-related medical conditions. Doctors also

What Type Are You?

There are three basic types of body structures, and a person's type can affect their risk for becoming obese. An ectomorph has a small body with long arms and legs. A mesomorph is well proportioned with heavy muscles. An endomorph is someone with a large body and short arms and legs. An endomorph may also have a round shape and extra fat. Endomorphs are the most likely to become obese, but they can control their weight with diet and exercise.

look at a person's waist-to-hip ratio. Or they may use an instrument called a caliper to measure the thickness of skin folds (excess fat) in various points on the body.

What Causes Obesity?

People often think that someone who is obese does not have the self-control needed to regulate their diet. But health experts increasingly view obesity as a disease. According to the American Obesity Association, "When there is too much body fat, the result is obesity. Obesity is not a sign of a person being out of control. It is a serious medical disease."[1]

Hunger Triggers

Our bodies do a good job of letting us know when our stomachs are empty. There are also ways that our bodies can be fooled into thinking we are hungry.

• Time of day can trigger hunger simply because we have become conditioned to eating at certain times every day, such as lunch at noon and dinner at six.

• Sight makes us hungry. When we see something delicious, our body anticipates having that food enter our system.

• Variety, such as craving something sweet at the end of a big meal, is also something that convinces us we are still hungry even when we are full, because it is a craving that has not been satisfied.

• Smell causes hunger because scent is a trigger that food is near. Similar to sight, it activates the appetite process.

• Eating a meal with many refined carbohydrates, such as white pasta, makes our blood sugar drop. This is a signal to our body that we are hungry and need to eat even if it has not been long since our last meal.

On the most basic level, obesity occurs when a person takes in more calories from the food they eat than they burn up in exercise. A calorie is the amount of energy or heat that it takes to raise the temperature of one gram (.04 oz) of water by one degree Celsius (1.8°F). Food contains calories. When that food is consumed, the body processes those calories through metabolism. Humans use the energy from calories for breathing, moving, and even thinking. Calories, or excess energy, are either used immediately or stored for future use within fat cells.

People who routinely take in more calories through their food than their bodies burn through activity accumulate those extra calories as fat. Over time, this extra accumulation of calories may lead to obesity.

Other factors such as genetics, a person's environment, and behavior contribute to obesity. Certain genetic mutations can cause compulsive eating or lead to imbalances in brain chemicals and body hormones that

Average Calorie Needs

The average adult needs approximately 2,000 calories a day in order for their body to run efficiently. For girls aged 9 to 13, experts recommend 1,600 to 2,000 calories daily. For boys in the same age group, 1,800 to 2,200 are needed each day. This number can vary according to age, level of daily activity, and gender. Many teenage boys between 15 and 18 years of age require 3,000 calories daily because of their growth rate and activity levels.

regulate food intake. Most genetic mutations that influence body weight are rare. Another condition, known as hypothyroidism, occurs when the thyroid gland does not produce enough thyroid hormone to properly regulate weight. Some people come from families where there is simply a genetic tendency to store fat. This tendency may have evolved in individuals over thousands of years as a way to protect themselves from starvation when food was not abundant.

A person's environment also can contribute to obesity. Advances in tools, transportation, and technology have decreased daily physical activity. Meanwhile, people have more and easier access to low-cost, high-fat foods. For someone already susceptible to weight gain, the modern lifestyle may be enough to cause obesity.

Some environments may even encourage overeating. Families with unhealthy eating habits often pass those habits on to their children, who may subsequently develop weight problems. Many people also use food as a way to cope with difficult emotions.

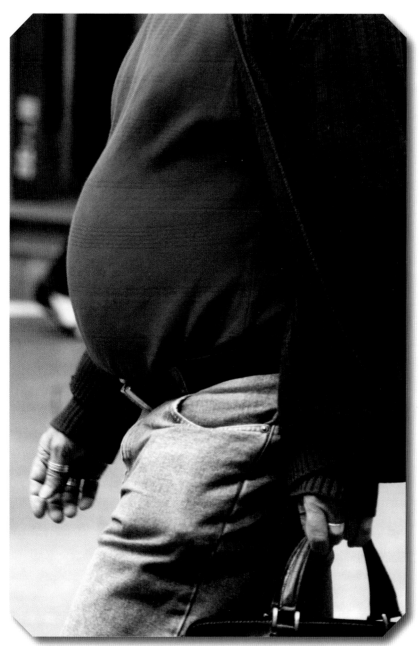

The modern lifestyle can contribute to obesity.

Ray A. Kroc, founder of McDonald's Corporation, started an era of fast food.

THE ERA OF SUPERSIZING

*I*n the 1930s and 1940s, if a family wanted to eat a meal at a restaurant, they would go to a diner or a family restaurant. Going out for a restaurant meal was a special occasion and not something done quickly. This changed with the creation of drive-in and fast-food restaurants in the late 1940s and 1950s. Suddenly, eating out became quick and convenient. Chain restaurants were built all over the country specializing in quick food that would be the same no matter what city you were in.

When fast-food restaurants first became popular, a typical meal was a reasonably sized portion. Average adults require 2,000 calories a day to fuel their bodies. A meal at McDonald's consisting of a regular hamburger (250 calories), a small order of french fries (250 calories), and a small soda (150 calories) would fall within a reasonable amount of calories for a single meal.

In the mid-1970s, fast-food restaurants began offering combination meals that grouped food items such as sandwiches, fries, and a drink together. They also added the option of "supersizing" a meal (increasing the size of the fries or drink, for example) for a little extra money. This yielded greater profits for the fast-food industry. But it also increased the portion size that the average American eater considered to be normal. A meal at McDonald's might mean a Big Mac (540 calories), large fries (570 calories), and a large soda (310 calories). The result is more than 1,400 calories in a single meal. That is more than half of the daily requirement for the average adult. It is nearly an entire day's worth of calories for the average middle school student.

SUPERSIZING THE AMERICAN DIET

Supersized portions of fast food seemed to culminate with the introduction of the "Monster Thickburger" by the Hardee's restaurant chain in November of 2004. This burger contained 1,420 calories. With the addition of a drink and fries, this meal would contain more calories and fat than most people should eat in an entire day. Nutrition experts instantly complained about the burger. The Center for Science in the Public Interest stated, "At a time of rampant heart disease and obesity, it is the height of corporate irresponsibility for a major chain to peddle a 1,420 calorie

Nutritional Facts

How does a Hardee's meal with the Monster Thickburger compare to a regular fast-food meal? The Monster Thickburger has 1,420 calories and 107 grams of fat. A large order of fries contains 610 calories and 28 grams of fat. Add a large Coke at 310 calories, and you have 2,330 calories and 135 grams of fat. Remember, the recommended daily allowance for the average adult for an entire day is 2,000 calories and 65 grams of fat. A fast-food meal with a regular-sized hamburger (310 calories, 12 grams fat), a small order of fries (390 calories, 19 grams fat), and a small Coke (150 calories) totals of 1,010 calories. It is still half the recommended daily allowance of calories. But it is well below the Monster Thickburger meal.

At 1,420 calories, Hardee's Monster Thickburger raised concerns among nutrition experts.

sandwich."[1] Late night talk show host and comedian Jay Leno joked that the Monster Thickburger, "actually comes in a little cardboard box shaped like a coffin."[2]

Not only was the fast-food industry encouraging its customers to eat larger portions of food that contained high amounts of fat, calories, and sugar, but fast food was available everywhere, even in schools, hospitals, and large discount stores such as Wal-Mart. Americans were no longer eating just three regular meals a day. Instead, they had developed a culture of snacking. Kids might stop by a fast-food chain after school for a snack of fries or a burger. They might order a pizza to eat while watching television at night. This contributes greatly to the rate of obesity in the country. Suddenly, unhealthy food was readily available and relatively inexpensive.

Fast food became a necessity for fast-paced life. Families with a hectic schedule of activities used fast food instead of traditional home-cooked meals, especially since it was formulated to be easily eaten without utensils and could be consumed in the car. In 1972, Americans spent $3 billion on fast food. By 2003, they were spending $110 billion. On any one day, one out of every four Americans visits a fast-food restaurant. And many people eat fast food for more than one meal a day.

The Cost of Coke

Soft drinks such as Coca-Cola are one of the most profitable items on the menu at a fast-food restaurant. McDonald's sells more Coke than anyone else in the world. According to Eric Schlosser's book, *Chew on This,* McDonald's buys the syrup at approximately $4.25 for a gallon (3.8 L) and adds carbonated water. A medium Coke that is priced at $1.29 might contain nine cents' worth of syrup, plus the cost of water and the cup. As Schlosser states in his book, "You can earn a lot of money selling sugar and water in a paper cup."[3]

"Fast Food Industry Has Wrecked My Life"

As Americans became increasingly health conscious, many people who suffered from health issues due to obesity began to blame fast food for their conditions. In July of 2002, New York resident Caesar Barber filed a lawsuit against McDonald's, Wendy's, Kentucky Fried Chicken, and Burger King. He weighed 272 pounds (123 kg), had suffered two heart attacks, and had diabetes. Barber claimed that the fast-food restaurants were responsible for his health problems. He had eaten food from these chain restaurants four or five times a week for 40 years and claimed he had never been told that this food was bad for his health. "Ads said '100 percent beef.' I thought that meant it was good for you," Barber told *Newsday* magazine. "[But] the fast food industry has wrecked my life."[4]

No More Disney Happy Meals

In May of 2006, Disney announced that it would be ending its ten-year deal with McDonald's restaurants to supply toys for McDonald's Happy Meals. Due to the increased concern over children, fast food, and obesity, Disney no longer wanted to be linked with McDonald's promotions. Health experts hoped that the end of the partnership would force McDonald's to make its food healthier, especially since that food is so heavily marketed to children.

According to Eric Schlosser, author of *Fast Food Nation*:

It will put more pressure on McDonald's to change what they sell in Happy Meals. The obesity issue would be irrelevant if the food in the Happy Meals was healthy.[5]

Take the Portion Quiz

Do you think you know how much portion sizes at fast-food restaurants have changed in the last 20 years? Take the Portion Distortion Quiz on the National Institute of Health Web site at http://hp2010.nhlbihin.net/portion/keep.htm. You can also see how much physical activity it takes to burn off the increased amount of calories in today's larger portions.

That same year, the parents of two teenage girls filed a lawsuit against McDonald's. They claimed that the fast-food company had failed to provide its customers with a list of the ingredients found in their food, especially the high levels of sugar, fat, salt, and cholesterol. The two girls suffered from obesity, heart disease, high blood pressure, and high cholesterol. They were frequent customers of McDonald's—as were their parents—and one of the girls claimed that she ate breakfast and dinner items at McDonald's every single day.

The fast-food companies argued in both cases that more factors are involved in obesity than just eating fast food, such as heredity, medical conditions, environment, and inactivity. Barber's case was thrown out of court. The judge in the case of the two teenage girls initially agreed with the fast-food companies, stating,

> *Where should the line be drawn between an individual's own responsibility to take care of herself and society's responsibility to ensure others shield her?*[6]

SUPERSIZE ME

In 2004, director Morgan Spurlock filmed a documentary called *Supersize Me: A Film of Epic Proportions.* Spurlock had seen news coverage of the two teenage girls whose parents sued McDonald's. While he agreed with the judge that obesity and fast food should be a case of personal responsibility, he was curious about the effects of so much fast food on a body. He decided to produce a documentary based on his experience of eating only McDonald's food for 30 consecutive days. He chose McDonald's because it was the world's largest fast-food chain and, at that time, accounted for more than 40 percent of all fast food served in the United States.

At the end of his 30-day experiment, Spurlock had gained 25 pounds (11 kg). He suffered from headaches, breathing problems, and chest pains. He was also depressed and tired. After the documentary was released, McDonald's removed the supersizing option from its menu.

While fast-food restaurants may contribute to the national weight problem, many people do not feel that the responsibility for the obesity epidemic lies solely with these businesses. Other factors in modern lifestyles contribute just as much in cultivating obesity. Many of these factors are directly related to the U.S. school system.

The Cheeseburger Bill

In 2004, the U.S. House of Representatives introduced the Personal Responsibility in Food Consumption Act, better known as the Cheeseburger Bill. The bill was intended to prevent people from suing fast-food restaurants on the grounds that they were liable for their customers' obesity and related health issues. The bill passed the House of Representatives but failed to pass in the Senate. Some states may be adopting their own versions of this bill in the future.

Michigan Supreme Court Justice Robert P. Young Jr.
does not like lawsuits filed against fast-food restaurants.
The Cheeseburger Bill would prevent such cases.

School cafeterias try to offer healthier choices on restricted budgets.

TEACHING OBESITY

In 1946, President Harry S. Truman
signed the National School Lunch Act in
an effort to improve the overall health of American
children. The act was intended to provide free
or low-cost meals to low-income schoolchildren.

It also focused on providing nutritionally sound cafeteria meals to all students. According to the act, "lunches served by schools participating in the school lunch program under this Act shall meet minimum nutritional requirements prescribed ... on the basis of tested nutritional research."[1] The menu requirements provided to schools by the National School Lunch Act and the U.S. Department of Agriculture were designed to meet one-half to one-third of the daily nutritional requirements of children ten to twelve years old. It also hoped to educate children about healthy, balanced diets.

Dollars and Cents

A few decades later, many school districts suffered budget cuts. In the 1980s and 1990s, less funding made it difficult for schools to provide lunch meals that were both healthy and appealing to kids. Many high schools had too many students and not enough money, so they adopted an open campus at lunchtime. The open campus policy allowed students to leave campus for lunch and then return for afternoon classes. But school lunch programs required money from students who were paying full price for their lunches. Based on household income, some students paid full price for school lunches, and other students had subsidized lunches. This meant that students from lower-income households did not pay full price for a school lunch. Extra money made from full-price lunches helped fund the lunch program. If students who paid full-price for school lunches did not want to eat cafeteria food, the school's lunch budget was negatively affected because it then had less money on which to operate. According to Karen Springen in a *Newsweek* article "Can Big Business Improve School Lunch?":

> *The federal government reimburses [a] school $2.32 for kids on the free-lunch program and $1.92 for kids on the reduced-price option. To subsidize healthy eating, the government also kicks in 22 cents per full-pay child, too. That's not a lot of money with which to make inexpensive, mass-produced, healthy lunches that kids want to eat.*[2]

Some schools coped by offering lunch menus that contained the same sorts of foods kids would eat at fast-food restaurants, such as pizza, burgers, french fries, and chicken nuggets. With the requirements of the National Lunch Program, however, it was difficult to make food taste good and still produce a lunch that contained less than 30 percent of its calories from fat and less than 10 percent from saturated fat. If kids did not like the food that was offered, they either would not buy school lunch or discard much of what was on their trays. Sometimes students went even further. In Rhode Island, the entire school lunch program was boycotted by students after deep-fried french fries were removed from the menu.

Budget problems and student preferences led many school districts to allow fast-food outlets such as McDonald's, Pizza Hut, and Subway to either operate inside the school or provide their products to school cafeterias. Approximately 19,000 schools in the United States now serve fast food in their cafeterias. With high-fat school lunches and fast food served to students, obesity rates among children and teens will most likely continue to rise.

An Average Lunch

The National School Lunch Act provided guidelines for what a typical, nutritionally balanced school lunch should contain. The guidelines were designed to meet one-third to one-half of a child's minimum daily nutritional requirements:
• Whole milk: one-half pint (237 ml)
• Protein-rich food consisting of any of the following or a combination thereof: fresh or processed meat, poultry meat, cheese, cooked or canned fish: two ounces (59 ml)
• Dry peas or beans or soybeans, cooked: half cup (118 ml)
• Peanut butter: four tablespoons (59 ml)
• Eggs: 1
• Raw, cooked, or canned vegetables or fruits, or both: three-fourths cup (177 ml)
• Bread, muffins, or hot bread made of whole grain cereal or enriched flour: 1 portion
• Fortified margarine or butter: two teaspoons (10 ml)

Vending Machines and Marketing Deals

In many schools, vending machines had been placed as part of a marketing deal with the company that manufactured the products inside the machines. The vending machines provided high-calorie sodas and high-fat snacks to students. Schools were reluctant to remove the machines because the products provided revenue. According to a Government Accounting Office (GAO) report:

> *Profits from soda vending machines generated several thousand dollars over a year's time to be used at the discretion of the principal. Some principals said it was their only funding source for expenditures such as awards, ... school or class field trips, and other educational opportunities.*[3]

The arrangements between school districts and vendors such as Coca-Cola and Pepsi were referred to as pouring contracts. Some schools agreed to sell only one

Liquid Candy

Soft drinks are one of the worst contributors to the obesity epidemic. Nutritionists call them "liquid candy" because one 12-ounce (355 ml) can of soda contains the equivalent of 14 teaspoons (69 ml) of sugar. Kids who drink soda are drinking it in place of more nutritious beverages such as milk. The amount of soda being consumed by kids has steadily risen. In 1978, a typical American teenage boy drank approximately seven ounces (207 ml) of soda every day. Now he drinks more than three times that amount.

*A student buys snacks from one of the vending machines
at Lane Tech High School in Chicago, Illinois.*

particular brand of soft drink and to post advertising around the school for that drink. In return, the school would receive a percentage of the soft drink sales as well as a yearly bonus payment that could be as much as $100,000. Schools also received free soft drinks to sell at school fund-raising events. For the beverage companies, the long-term goal of these programs was to increase soft drink consumption of students by as much as 75 percent. Students began to drink more soft drinks instead of healthier beverages such as milk, fruit juice, or water.

Beyond unbalanced lunch programs and vending machines, there have been other ways that schools have possibly contributed to rising obesity rates. School fundraisers have sold high-calorie snacks and drinks to raise money for school projects and events. Many schools have felt that it would be difficult to raise enough money if they sold healthier foods. Teachers have also used food items such as cookies or candy as rewards for good classroom behavior or for scoring well on tests or projects.

A Pepsi Shirt on a Coca-Cola Day

In March of 1998, high school student Mike Cameron was suspended from Greenbrier High School for wearing a shirt with a Pepsi logo during the school's Coca-Cola Education Day. The school was competing in a nationwide contest. The school with the most creativity in distributing Coca-Cola cards (a promotional card featuring discounts at several area businesses) would win $10,000. Greenbrier invited Coca-Cola executives to be guest speakers in classrooms and arranged for the entire student body to be photographed spelling out the word "Coke." Mike arrived for the picture in a shirt that plainly displayed the Pepsi logo. He received a day of in-school suspension. His story became news around the world, including national newspapers, news programs, and radio shows. Pepsi sent him a supply of Pepsi shirts and hats.

It is programs and incentives such as this that have many parents, educators, and health officials concerned. If schools are promoting the consumption of high-calorie, low-nutritional beverages such as Coke and Pepsi, what are students learning about healthy food choices? Can students make informed choices if they are given a mixed message that it is wrong to take a stand against junk food marketing giants? Or are these giants helping schools by finding methods of additional funding?

What Happened to Gym Class?

In addition to the problem of producing school lunches that are nutritious and appealing, schools have also struggled with a decline in physical education (PE), or gym class. In many schools, physical education requirements have been reduced or eliminated. In most high schools, juniors and seniors are no longer required to take physical education classes. Some students are only required to take one year of gym. According to an article published by the Parent Teacher Association (PTA):

> Just during the past decade, the number of U.S. high school students attending daily physical education classes dropped from 42 to 29 percent. Currently, nearly half of all students and 75 percent of high school students do not attend any physical education classes ... Schools cut gym classes for lack of funding, but more often cuts resulted

Fast-food Incentives

In addition to pouring contracts, fast food, candy, and beverage companies have found other ways to market their products to children through schools. Pizza Hut sponsors the "Book It" program, where children read for a certain number of minutes and are rewarded with coupons for free personal-sized pizzas. McDonald's supplies free educational materials to schools, such as nutritional curricula. Children may learn math using Tootsie Rolls, M&M's, and Domino's Pizza materials. All of these methods place the company logos and products where kids will see them every day.

from time constraints that develop with the addition of new curriculum. [4]

Time and money constraints have caused many schools to eliminate recess. This reduces children's daily physical activity even further. Some schools claim that they have stopped including recess in students' schedules because of safety and supervision concerns. But critics say the cuts have been due to an expanding academic curriculum.

It seems like modern schools, faced with budget problems and lack of time, have played a major role in the increasing obesity of their students. Students themselves, however, appreciate being able to eat what they like and not spending time in required gym classes. Some people ask, then, do obesity and its effects matter? In a culture where more people are becoming overweight, just what are the consequences of obesity on health and society? Is there more to the issue of obesity than just looking good?

Commercials

Companies that manufacture fast foods and snack foods have found another way to make their presence known in the classroom. Channel One is a commercial television network. It provides free television sets for classrooms, but children must watch two minutes of advertisements every day. Many school districts with no money for technology or equipment accept the terms, even though the network exposes students to more food advertisements.

*Once standard throughout schools,
physical education classes have been significantly cut back.*

Some children, such as 12-year-old Yervant Artin, have the adult form of diabetes.

OBESITY AND HEALTH

ociety often thinks of obesity only in terms of appearance, since overweight and obese people do not fit media images of the perfect body type. But obesity is much more serious than whether or not someone looks like a fashion model.

The CDC indicates that the number of deaths from obesity-related illnesses (approximately 400,000 deaths in 2000) is fast approaching the number of deaths from tobacco. This makes obesity the underlying cause of more than 16 percent of deaths in the United States.

The CDC assembled statistics relating obesity to increased risks for specific diseases. In a study posted in January of 2003, the CDC stated:

> *Compared to adults with healthy weight, those [adults who are considered overweight or obese] had an increased risk of being diagnosed with diabetes (7.37 times greater), high blood pressure (6.38 times greater), high cholesterol levels (1.88 times greater), asthma (2.72 times greater), and arthritis (4.41 times greater).* [1]

Health problems related to being overweight or obese affect more than those struggling with the disease. In order to treat the increasing number of people experiencing health problems related to obesity, health care costs increase for everyone in society, including those who are healthy. In the debate over obesity, the issue of how to manage its health and social costs is at the center of the argument. But what are those health and social costs?

Obesity and the Heart

The greatest risks faced by overweight or obese people are high blood pressure and heart disease. Blood pressure is the force of blood pushing against the walls of the arteries as the heart pumps that blood. High blood pressure makes the heart work harder than it should. It can lead to congestive heart failure in which the heart can no longer pump blood properly. High blood pressure damages the arteries and may harden or scar them. Hardened arteries are less effective at supplying the necessary blood to organs throughout the body. High blood pressure forces the kidneys to work harder at cleaning the blood in the body. Eventually, the kidneys may shut down.

Heart disease is the general term used to describe any disorder that does not allow the heart to function normally. Often, heart disease is related to high blood-fat levels, specifically fats known as triglycerides and cholesterol. Both fats are essential to the

The Fat Five

Nutritionists have developed a list of the top five factors that contribute to obesity among Americans:

1. increased portion sizes
2. lack of physical activity
3. marketing targeted at children
4. increasing amounts of corn syrup and other sweeteners in foods
5. consumer demand for prepared foods with long shelf lives

body in normal amounts, but too much of either is unhealthy. Cholesterol can accumulate and clog arteries. This makes the heart work harder to pump blood. Ultimately, the clogged arteries cause a heart attack, as the blood supply to the heart becomes blocked or cut off.

OBESITY AND DIABETES

As serious as heart disease and high blood pressure are, obesity is also responsible for the alarming increase in the incidents of type 2 diabetes in the United States. Diabetes results from an imbalance in the way the body uses sugar. Insulin is a hormone produced by the body. It helps regulate the amount of glucose, or sugar, in the blood. In type 1 diabetes, the body does not produce insulin to properly manage glucose in the blood and deliver it to the body's cells. So, people with type 1 diabetes must always take insulin. Type 2 diabetes, however, occurs when the body can no longer produce enough insulin to keep blood glucose levels normal. This happens because there is too much glucose coming into the body. Eventually, the body loses its ability to keep up and becomes insulin resistant. This results in high blood sugar because there is not enough insulin to take glucose to the places in the body where it is needed. Too much glucose in the blood can lead to a diabetic coma and eventually death, unless the disease is treated in its early stages.

People who are overweight or obese have a higher risk of developing type 2 diabetes. Obese people are three to five times more likely to suffer from diabetes than people of normal weight. Also, type 2 diabetes has a higher heritability, meaning the risk of developing the disease is greater in some families than others. Type 2 diabetes used to be considered an adult disease. Until very recently, it was rarely diagnosed in children. Type 1 diabetes used to be called "juvenile onset diabetes" because it was the form of the disease most often

Leptin

In 1994, a researcher at Rockefeller University discovered a hormone called leptin. This hormone acts as a signal from fat cells to the brain, telling it that the body has had enough food. In laboratory animals with a deficiency of leptin, their brains determined their bodies were still hungry even after the animals had eaten. This deficiency led to overeating and weight gain. A person with normal weight produces more leptin as his or her body fat increases. This helps reduce appetite and prevent weight gain. If body fat decreases in a normal person, the amount of leptin also decreases. This signals the body to take in more food. While most obese people have enough leptin, researchers believe that overweight or obese people do not respond to leptin signals. If people's brains are resistant to the action of this hormone, their bodies do not get the message that they have had enough to eat.

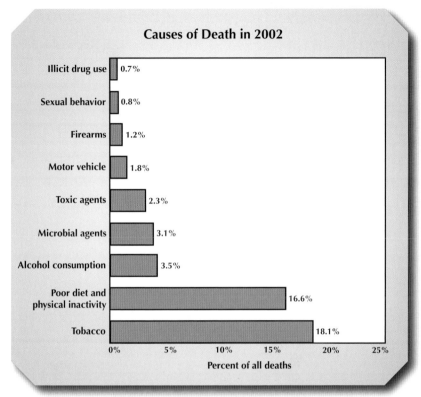

Causes of Death in 2002

Cause	Percent of all deaths
Illicit drug use	0.7%
Sexual behavior	0.8%
Firearms	1.2%
Motor vehicle	1.8%
Toxic agents	2.3%
Microbial agents	3.1%
Alcohol consumption	3.5%
Poor diet and physical inactivity	16.6%
Tobacco	18.1%

Poor diet and inadequate exercise are second only to tobacco use as causes of death.

diagnosed in childhood. Now, with so many obese children, type 2 is the most common type of diabetes diagnosed in adolescents. This disease can result in serious side effects such as blindness, amputation of limbs, and kidney disease. It is one of the most potentially harmful diseases in terms of both health and health care costs.

Obesity and Cancer

Obesity also may be a contributing factor to many forms of cancer. Cancer is a condition where the unregulated growth of cancer cells eventually takes over and destroys the body. Researchers who have evaluated cancer deaths over a period of 15 years conclude that more than 90,000 cancer deaths are linked to excess body weight. In a study conducted for the American Institute of Cancer Research, obesity expert Dr. George Bray states,

> *The more we understand about obesity, the more we realize that simply being overweight and inactive—in other words, living the modern American lifestyle—produces basic hormonal and metabolic changes [that] make it easier for cancer to gain a foothold.*[2]

According to Dr. Bray's research, fat cells secrete a wide variety of hormones and other growth factors in the blood, which send signals to other parts of the body. Usually this signals the body's cells to grow in a controlled manner. But the excess fat in an obese person may trigger those same cells to grow at an unusually rapid rate. The risk for developing cancer increases as body weight increases. Obesity also makes diagnosing and treating cancer more difficult

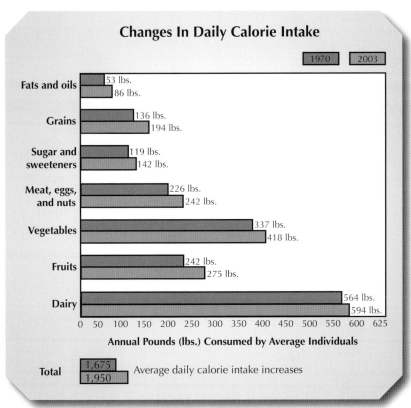

Changes In Daily Calorie Intake

| | 1970 | 2003 |

Category	1970	2003
Fats and oils	53 lbs.	86 lbs.
Grains	136 lbs.	194 lbs.
Sugar and sweeteners	119 lbs.	142 lbs.
Meat, eggs, and nuts	226 lbs.	242 lbs.
Vegetables	337 lbs.	418 lbs.
Fruits	242 lbs.	275 lbs.
Dairy	564 lbs.	594 lbs.

Annual Pounds (lbs.) Consumed by Average Individuals

| Total | 1,675 | 1,950 | Average daily calorie intake increases |

In 1970, the average individual consumed significantly fewer calories per day, or pounds of food per year, than did the average individual in 2003.

because the excess body fat makes it difficult to find tumors (cancerous growths). Once an obese person is diagnosed, it can be more difficult to treat cancer since medication such as chemotherapy is absorbed by fat. An obese person with cancer has a less likely chance of successful treatment than a person of normal body weight.

Other Health Risks

In addition to high blood pressure, heart disease, and cancer, obesity is linked to many other painful and even life-threatening diseases. Obese people often suffer from arthritis due to the strain from carrying excess weight. Obese people are more likely to suffer from carpal tunnel syndrome. They also suffer from conditions such as blood clots, hernias, menstrual disorders, infertility, complications during pregnancy, and respiratory problems. These ailments require more frequent medical attention and ultimately result in higher health insurance and medical costs for everyone. The ailments also take a tremendous toll on the quality of life for obese individuals and their families. Aside from the physical aspects of obesity, what are the mental and psychological impacts for people who are overweight and obese? Are those risks just as great?

Toxic Food?

According to Dr. Kelly Brownell, Americans live in a toxic food environment. Americans are endlessly confronted by fast-food restaurants, food advertisements on television, and tempting displays of candy at store checkout lanes. The toxic food environment in the United States has spread to other countries such as China as they adopt American habits and foods.

Researchers such as Reza Hakkak study
the relationship between obesity and cancer.

One of the emotional struggles of being overweight is size discrimination.

Obesity and Mental Health

Some overweight or obese people are discriminated against because of their size. Constant ridicule may be just as negative to an obese person's psychological well-being as the potential physical problems are to his or her physical health.

The emotional costs of obesity are also a social concern. Because the mental, psychological, and social stigmas of being obese during childhood are so serious, many people believe the government needs to address the mental health aspect of obesity as well as the physical aspect.

"I Wanted to Be Dead"

Overweight children often face teasing, bullying, and higher rates of depression. A Yale University and University of Hawaii at Manatoa study in 2007 found that obese children's quality of life was similar to children who had cancer. The study found that overweight kids faced stigmas and bias in many aspects of life, from school and the media to parents, educators, and other children. As one of the almost 15 percent of teens who are considered overweight or obese, Lisa was teased and ridiculed at school to the point of saying that she would kill herself if she had to return. Lisa describes how she felt:

> *I wanted to be dead. The prospect of being teased for being fat every day of my life just made me shut down emotionally. I went through the motions but my grades were poor and I was just plain numb most of the time. No one really knew how awful it was. Not even me.*[1]

Lisa entered a support group for overweight teens and has begun to lose weight, but her story is typical of what many overweight or obese people face, especially in the vulnerable teen years. Many overweight and obese children and teens face constant teasing, taunting, and poor treatment from other schoolchildren, their community, and even their family. This often leads to depression and other psychological conditions, including suicidal tendencies. The article "The Psychological Consequences of Obesity in Children and Teens" reports:

> *A recent survey reveals that obese children rate their quality of life as low as those of young cancer patients undergoing chemotherapy. Other studies are reporting increased rates of depression, low self-esteem, and social isolation. ... As these children grow up, they are less likely to be accepted into college, less likely to get married, and more likely to occupy a lower socio-economic status.* [2]

In a society where thin is seen as beautiful, the emotional costs of obesity can be much harder to deal with than the potential for life-threatening medical conditions. The emotional pain affects obese teens and obese adults.

OBESITY AND DISCRIMINATION

As hard as it is for overweight and obese people to go through teasing and ridicule for their weight, there are other aspects of obesity that are affected more than mental and physical health. Obese people are often discriminated against in the workplace, as well as in many other situations. "Weight stigma" is the formal term for the negative attitudes that people have toward obese people and how it affects their interpersonal interactions and activities. Weight stigma comes in several different forms. These include verbal, physical, and other barriers of bias based on people's size. Weight stigma often leads to

The Personal Story of an Obese Teen

I'm seventeen years old and I weigh 440 pounds. I've been overweight since I was twelve years old. I used to go to school but I had to drop out because people continued to make fun of me. I suffer from depression, anxiety and agoraphobia. I hate my body so much and I wish I could lose this weight in a heartbeat, but I can't. I missed my whole teenage-hood because of my obesity. I wish I could go into a store and buy sexy clothing and bell-bottoms and tank tops and a bikini, but I can't because they don't make clothing in my size. You know what, I feel so guilty for letting myself get so big and I wish I could just live an ordinary teenage life, and have cute boys look at me and not pick on me, because I would be beautiful. And I could go out and enjoy life instead of being afraid all the time.[3]

—from the "My Story" section of the American Obesity Association Web site

discrimination, such as in an employment situation. Obese or overweight people who experience weight stigma have higher rates of depression, anxiety, low self-esteem, and social isolation. Weight stigmatization is especially difficult for children and adolescents. Teens are more likely to be depressed, withdrawn, and even suicidal.

Overweight and obese people can face discrimination in employment situations such as hiring and promotions because of their weight. They are stereotyped as having emotional problems, social problems, or negative personality traits for no reason other than their appearance. One study found that white women who were mildly obese were paid 5.9 percent less than similar (aged or ethnicity) women who were not obese. Women that were morbidly obese were paid 24 percent less than their normal-weight coworkers. An obese woman remembers her search for jobs, saying,

> My real problems started when I looked for employment. Any time I would go to look for work in an office setting, they would say the job has been filled. Unless the person doing the hiring was also overweight.[4]

The American Obesity Association notes:

Some people such as Peggy Lucas, seen here at a Weight Watchers support meeting, battle weight their entire lives.

> *Obesity is often described as the last "acceptable" form of discrimination based on physical appearance. ... Evidence of discrimination is found at virtually every stage of the employment cycle, including selection, placement, compensation, promotion, discipline, and discharge.*[5]

Employers may also penalize overweight or obese employees financially due to the increasing cost of health insurance for corporations. Thinner employees generally have lower health insurance costs, which ultimately saves the company money. Companies are encouraging their employees

Boarding Schools

The Academy of the Sierras (AOS) in California is a residential school for children and adolescents ages 11 to 18. The school has been extremely successful in helping its students lose weight. In many cases, students who remain enrolled for at least two semesters decreased their obesity by 60 percent. The school combines academics and healthy eating with therapeutic programs. Students usually achieve higher academic performance, better self-esteem and behavior, and a higher level of fitness than they had previously attained. Best yet, students do not experience the teasing and stigmatization that obese kids often experience in public schools. Students have also shown the ability to maintain their weight once they leave the school.

to lose weight and often offer incentives to those who do. Those who are unable to lose the weight may experience shame or discouragement by their employer.

There are very few laws against obesity discrimination. Only the state of Michigan has a law banning discrimination on the basis of weight.

OTHER LIMITATIONS OF OBESITY

Weight may also affect travelers. Airlines sometimes require obese passengers to purchase two tickets if the traveler needs two seats to accommodate his or her size. Some airlines claim that the increasing weight of passengers has been responsible for the rising costs of airline travel in general. The airlines argue that it takes more fuel to power the aircraft off the runway when there is more weight added to the plane.

Overweight and obese people also face challenges in their own vehicles. Car manufacturers are only required to provide seatbelts that can restrain a person up to six feet (1.8 m) tall and weighing 215 pounds (98 kg). Petitions have been filed with the National Highway Traffic Safety Administration to require manufacturers to make seat belt extenders available to larger people and to make longer seatbelts an option for the car buyer at the time of purchase.

Extremely obese people have also suffered from limitations in settings such as restaurants and movie theaters. Their increased size makes it difficult to accommodate them in standard sized chairs and theater seats. In the late 1980s, Olive Garden restaurants outfitted every location in their chain with at least three chairs that could accommodate larger customers. This was done after a complaint was made by a customer that could not fit comfortably into any of the chairs or booths at his local restaurant.

THE PRICE OF OBESITY

If the overall cost of obesity in terms of both emotional and physical health is so high, and the

Shaq's Challenge

In the summer of 2007, a new television show debuted on the ABC network. Starring Shaquille O'Neal, the show was called *Shaq's Big Challenge*. It involved the selection of six obese children who would work with Shaq and his team of doctors, fitness experts, and nutritionists to lose weight and change their lifestyles. Not only did Shaq hope to help these six children lose weight, but he also hoped to use his celebrity influence on issues such as mandatory physical education classes in schools.

percentage of obese people is steadily increasing, what can be done? Many people feel that obesity can only be addressed through public health, legislation, and large-scale social programs. As one person posted on the American Obesity Association Web site,

> *We should all ... hope that America gets wise and see what obesity is doing to us. I worry for the young people to come. We need to educate more doctors and insurance companies about this deadly disease. Help teachers and mentors learn to understand how it feels to be overweight. Maybe we can stop the cycle for the next generation.*[6]

With all of these financial, physical, and emotional costs, the obesity epidemic has raised a national debate: Does responsibility lie with society or the individual? And what steps should be taken to deal with obesity and prevent it as well?

*While increased activity can help fight obesity,
other options such as food legislation are part of the obesity debate.*

Arkansas Governor Mike Huckabee, left, talks with Indian Hills Elementary School students in North Little Rock, Arkansas.

LEGISLATING OUR DIETS

here is very little argument when it comes to recognizing that obesity is a serious medical condition that can result in both physical and psychological health concerns. The arguments arise over deciding who is ultimately responsible for keeping Americans healthy and reversing the rising rate of obesity. Many officials feel that this health crisis has reached a point where it can no longer be left to the individual to manage his or her own health choices.

What Is a Government to Do?

The United States government is already involved in trying to reduce obesity rates, particularly since the cost of obesity in terms of health insurance and treatment affects every taxpayer. The federal government pays for approximately half of the $100 billion in annual medical bills related to health complications from obesity. This makes it both an economic and a social problem for the government. According to the CDC, "One of the national health objectives for 2010 is to reduce the prevalence of obesity among adults to less than 15 percent."[1]

Most of the government programs meant to combat obesity focus on public health education. These programs try to shift the public's perception away from obesity as an issue of appearance and toward the idea that obesity is a serious health matter. Public education programs emphasize healthy eating and portion control as well as the importance of exercise and a less-sedentary lifestyle. Schools are being encouraged to reinstate mandatory physical education classes at every grade level. Currently, only an approximate 25 percent of teens participate in gym classes.

Vending Machines

Several senators have pushed for a law allowing the United States Department of Agriculture to regulate the contents of vending machines just as they do the federal lunch program. Because schools are funded through taxes, some people feel it is the government's responsibility to step in.

A 2004 survey showed that the junk food sold in school vending machines competes with, and usually undermines, the healthy foods sold in school lunches. A study of 1,420 vending machines in 251 middle and high schools showed that 75 percent of the drinks and 85 percent of the snacks were of poor nutritional value. Of all beverages in vending machines, 70 percent were soft drinks and other sugary drinks. Only 5 percent were milk, usually whole milk or 2 percent milk rather than 1 percent or skim. Of the snacks sold in these vending machines, 42 percent were candy, 25 percent were chips, and 13 percent were baked goods.

While nutritional concerns have led some schools to ban the sale of soda and junk food in vending machines, many more schools still rely on these machines for revenue. Kids are still using them to create their lunches from unhealthy choices.

The U.S. government is also trying to encourage schools to use healthier lunch menus that include more fruits, vegetables, and whole grains. Public education programs advise adults to get more exercise, stressing the need for at least 30 minutes every day. Employers and communities are also encouraged to provide more exercise opportunities and safe public recreation facilities. Government public education programs, however, may not be enough to persuade Americans to eat better and to get more exercise.

Some researchers feel that the government should implement taxes on unhealthy foods such as chips, candy, and soft drinks. A "junk food" tax is already being considered in countries such as Australia and England. Many unhealthy foods are often cheaper than healthy foods. This tax would help correct the cost imbalance and may convince people to eat healthier foods. Other experts argue that this would harm low-income families who rely on inexpensive, high-fat foods. Others support allowing health insurance providers to charge obese people a higher premium than people who maintain a healthy weight.

Food Policing: Legislating Change

What is the next step that government can take for those who do not follow guidelines and recommendations? On both state and national levels, lawmakers are beginning to pass legislation to combat the obesity problem. In December of 2003, Congress passed the Improved Nutrition and

Physical Activity Act (IMPACT). This act authorizes implementing various government activities that are designed to prevent, diagnose, and treat obesity. These activities include training for health professionals in treating and preventing obesity, giving grants to communities for promoting physical activity, funding studies into the causes of obesity and the effectiveness of weight loss program and drugs, and promoting physical activity through television campaigns and other media.

In 2005, legislators in the state of New Jersey introduced a bill to limit vending machine sales in schools:

> *[Four combined bills in legislation] would prohibit the sale of foods of minimal nutritional value to pupils at public elementary or middle schools until at least one-half hour after the end of the school day. Before school opens and*

Obesity Advocate Groups

Like any group of people with concerns and shared interests, there are support and advocacy groups for obese people. One of the most vocal is the National Association to Advance Fat Acceptance (NAAFA). NAAFA's primary focus is not weight reduction. Rather, the group advocates for the rights of overweight and obese people. The association urges society to accept people as they are. NAAFA argues that fat does not necessarily mean that a person is unhealthy, and it is better to focus on a personal level of fitness than on being thin.

during school hours, vending machine food sold to pupils would have to be a whole grain, enriched or fortified grain or grain product, a fruit or vegetable, a nut or nut spread, a seed, a legume, a trail mix, a soy-based product, a milk or dairy product, an electrolyte-replacement beverage, 100 percent real fruit or vegetable juice, or water. ... Vending machines in high schools would have to contain at least one food and one beverage item which meets this dietary criteria.[2]

Legislation has been introduced to increase the required number of hours of physical education in schools. Legislation has also been introduced that would require restaurants to post the fat and calorie content of their menu items. In September of 2006, New York City unveiled a proposed ban on the use of artificial trans-fatty acids such as partially hydrogenated oils. Many bakery goods, frozen foods such as pizza and toaster pastries, and french fries contain trans fats. Trans fats are unhealthy even in fairly small amounts and are a leading cause of heart disease. Under the proposal, any restaurant using trans fats would have to switch to a healthier alternative or risk fines of $200 to $2,000. A spokesperson for the Center for Science in the Public Interest remarked, "This move sets an important precedent and has far–reaching health implications. We expect other cities and states will follow."[3]

TRACKING OBESITY IN SCHOOLS

Some states have taken steps toward recognizing and preventing obesity in their schools. In 2003, Arkansas began tracking children's weight in school. New Hampshire began a similar program that year. Volunteers recorded children's heights and weights and calculated body mass index (BMI) to determine if the students were overweight. According to the information collected by the schools, 18 percent of the girls and 22 percent of the boys were overweight or obese. This was higher than the national average of 16 percent. Children were also tested for their level of physical fitness.

The program was designed to identify children at risk for obesity or who were already overweight. "We're trying to do this to show them their fitness

The New Food Pyramid

During the twentieth century, the federal government created different ways to instruct people about balanced diets. These methods include the four food groups. The four food groups were replaced with a food pyramid as a way to promote healthy eating. Based on the government's dietary guidelines, it was meant to be an easy way for people to balance their diets. In 2005, the government replaced the old food pyramid with a new one called MyPyramid. The new pyramid places an emphasis on eating a variety of foods, including healthy fats, and engaging in physical activity.

*MyPyramid, released in 2005, has placed an emphasis
on physical activity as well as a balanced diet.*

level and de-emphasize their body shape and size,"
said Dr. Walter Hoerman, a pediatrician who helped
lead efforts to improve children's health in the
New Hampshire program.[4] After realizing that they
were out of shape, some students made an effort
to exercise more and change their eating habits.
Students were also able to take an elective health class
that taught them about nutrition and food groups
and emphasized ways to get more exercise.

The University of Missouri cafeteria is one of many
to offer healthy alternatives for students.

While some parents appreciated the schools'
efforts at making health a priority, others felt the
program was an invasion of privacy. According to
a health specialist with the National Middle School
Association,

> Some districts have tried to include a letter home saying, "Your
> son or daughter is X number of pounds over the norm" and
> that has not been well-received. Parents were offended because
> they thought the schools were being invasive and not kind to
> their children.[5]

Many students were self-conscious about the process of being weighed and having other students ask them how much they weighed. Despite opposition, other states have followed Arkansas and New Hampshire and incorporated BMI and fitness testing into their curriculum. This often occurs along with new rules about what can be sold in school vending machines and at bake sales, candy sales, and other traditional fundraisers. A Texas senator proposed a law that would add a "weight grade" to a student's report card to indicate a student's BMI and whether the child was overweight or obese.

While these measures are not always popular with students and parents, groups such as the American Obesity Association support weight evaluation and nutrition programs in schools: "Outside of the home, children and adolescents spend the majority of their time in school. So, it makes sense that schools provide an environment that promotes healthy nutrition and physical activity habits."[6]

The Million Pound March

On August 15, 1998, hundreds of overweight people gathered in Santa Monica, California, for the Million Pound March. Organized by NAAFA, the march was a rally to let overweight people celebrate their identities and stand up against discrimination in society. Celebrities spoke about size discrimination in Hollywood and other areas of society and how overweight people needed to celebrate their individuality.

Who Is Ultimately Responsible?

Opposition to government laws and school programs designed to combat obesity shows that for many people obesity is not something to be legislated. To these opponents, eating habits and weight control are private matters, not public. It is up to the individual to manage his or her weight and nutrition. Many people do not want the government dictating what they can and cannot eat by controlling what foods are available. But as the percentage of obese children and adults continues to climb, others feel it has already been demonstrated that personal responsibility fails to keep most people at a healthy weight. These people believe the government should step in to protect us from ourselves. Should weight control remain the responsibility of the individual?

Reality Television

On the reality show, *The Biggest Loser*, overweight and obese contestants compete to see who can lose the most weight. The winner receives $250,000. Viewers can visit the show's Web site and have an expert assess their diets. Although the show states that weight loss is done in a healthy manner, contestants lose unnaturally large amounts of weight through constant exercise, a restricted diet, and dehydration, all of which are not encouraged methods for weight loss. The emphasis is on weight loss rather than maintaining that loss through changes in everyday lifestyle. Most contestants regain their weight after returning to their regular routines, as many are unable to maintain the extreme weight-loss methods used on the show.

Capitol Hill, Washington, D.C.

Exercise and diet are the only proven strategies for long-term maintenance of a healthy weight.

MAKING OUR
OWN CHANGES

F or the average person who wants to lose weight, there are many options, including diets, exercise routines, behavior therapy, special foods, drugs, and surgery. Researchers and obesity experts believe the one way to lose weight and keep it off is through diet and exercise. It is one of the best ways to maintain a healthy weight for your entire life. To lose weight, a person needs to take in fewer calories than they burn through exercise.

The diet and fitness industry is an enormous moneymaker. Dieting has become a multimillion-dollar business, with many different diets, diet books, and weight loss programs. These range from well-known programs that combine diets with a support group or counselors, such as Weight Watchers and Jenny Craig, to fad diets, such as the Atkins diet and the Ornish diet. Many diets promise fast results through certain combinations of foods or avoiding certain types of foods. While these diets may initially work, once the dieter is no longer following the special requirements, they may regain the weight.

Many dieters look for a quick fix—a combination of foods that will melt fat away without self-control. In his book, *Fat Land: How Americans Became the Fattest People in the World*, Greg Critzer states:

> *Completely missing from the new [diet book] genre was one increasingly strange and distant concept: self-control. No, it was all a matter of using nutritional science to "trick" the body into doing what it should be doing anyway.[1]*

Experts agree, however, that diets simply do not work for some people. Some people's bodies maintain a certain weight and level of fat, which is referred to as the body's set point. If these people decrease the amount of food they eat, their bodies automatically burn fewer calories. This makes it nearly impossible to lose weight.

Changing Bad Habits

Diets and exercise routines that incorporate behavior modification stand the best chance for long-term weight loss. Behavior modification works to change habits. To achieve weight loss, this may include adding simple exercise to daily routines, such as taking the stairs instead of an elevator and parking farther out in a parking lot.

Professional psychologists who specialize in eating disorders operate more formal behavior modification programs. These programs treat obesity as a disorder that can be managed with education. They teach obese patients to monitor how many calories they are eating. They also teach techniques such as eating slowly or only eating in a certain place in the house, such as the dining room or the kitchen. Experts may also treat some of the emotional problems that often are related to overeating and obesity, such as depression or anxiety.

A MAGIC PILL?

For people who diet unsuccessfully or who do not want to follow a diet and exercise regimen, diet pills and supplements are another option. These range from over-the-counter appetite suppressants to prescription medications for the severely obese.

Several types of diet drugs are on the market. Most weight-loss medications work by reducing appetite or the amount of food that is absorbed in the small intestine. Purgatives empty the intestines to keep food from being absorbed. Diuretics encourage the body to lose water, but they are ineffective for anything other than water weight loss. And stimulants suppress the appetite. Each type of drug has its own side effects and can become addictive. Many lose their effectiveness over time.

Prescription weight loss drugs, such as Meridia, are also available. Meridia is an appetite suppressant, thus it works by reducing hunger. Meridia can increase blood pressure and heart rate. Xenical is the trade name for the drug orlistat. This drug works by reducing the amount of calories from food that is absorbed during digestion. It blocks the body's absorption of approximately a third of the fats in food. This fat passes through the digestive system instead of being stored in the body. The use of this drug may cause gastrointestinal upsets for many people.

Amphetamines were popular weight loss drugs until the early 1970s, when tighter restrictions were placed on their use. They not only reduced a person's appetite, making it easy to lose weight, but they also made the patient feel good. These, too, have serious side effects, such as sleeplessness, increased heart rate and blood

The Newest Diet Drug

One of the newest diet drugs to be approved by the FDA is Alli, an over-the-counter version of the drug Xenical. Alli reduces the body's absorption of fat by approximately 25 percent. It can also have some embarrassing and uncomfortable side effects if not used properly. If the patient eats too much fat, they may experience oily discharges, uncontrollable bowel movements, and gas. The marketing information for the drug encourages users to wear dark pants and carry a change of clothing in case they have an accident. Alli comes with a diet plan and a Web site where users can track their progress, talk with other users, and consult a pharmacist or a nutritionist.

pressure, dizziness, hallucinations, seizures, psychiatric disorders, and sudden death. Also, larger and larger doses were required to continue weight loss as the drug lost effectiveness over time. This led to addiction and withdrawal problems.

In addition to prescription diet pills, herbal supplements are available in drugstores and health food stores without a prescription. The Food and Drug Administration (FDA) does not regulate these remedies in the same way as prescription drugs. However, they can have potentially life-threatening side effects. In 2004, the FDA banned the sale of ephedrine, an herbal supplement, used for both

Dangerous Drugs

The weight loss drug fen-phen was found to have potentially deadly side effects. Made of a combination of fenfluramine and phentermine, the drug was an appetite suppressant. Researchers hoped that by combining the two drugs, lower and safer doses of each could be used. By 1996, more than 18 million prescriptions had been written for fen-phen before studies discovered that one-third of its users developed heart valve disease. Fen-phen was taken off the market in 1997.

One of the most dangerous diet drugs ever used is DNP, officially known as 2,4-dinitrophenol. DNP was first experimented with as a diet drug in the 1920s, when scientists used it on mice and found it increased their metabolism by 50 to 300 percent. This increased metabolism caused the animals to run a fever, often resulting in death. Although the dosage was reduced for humans, DNP still caused high fevers and even death in some people. In addition to ephedra, amphetamines, and diuretics, DNP is an excellent example of a diet drug that is not worth the risk.

weight loss and as a decongestant. The herb produced high blood pressure, irregular heartbeat, strokes, and even death, especially when combined with caffeine.

While many hope that weight loss medication will be a quick and easy way to lose weight, research shows that most people regain their lost weight as soon as they stop taking the drug.

THE ULTIMATE WEIGHT LOSS TOOL

For obese patients who have not had success with diets or prescription medications, there is the option of surgery. Since the 1950s, doctors have been performing surgeries to help patients lose weight. Early surgeries removed portions of a patient's small intestine, which decreased the number of calories that could be absorbed into the body and resulted in weight loss. The intestinal bypass was popular for two decades, despite complications such as malnutrition, vomiting, and liver damage.

Gastric bypass surgery has become preferred to intestinal bypass. This surgery uses stainless steel staples, stitches, or plastic or metal bands to reduce the size of the stomach, and a bypass is done to connect the lower small intestine to this small

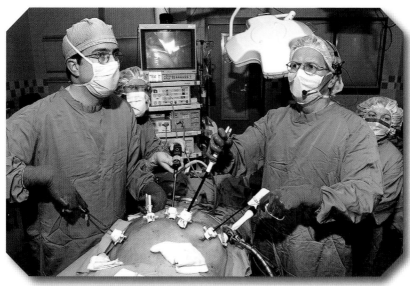

Gastric bypass surgery is often a last resort for weight loss.

stomach pouch. Food passes directly from the upper part of the stomach to the intestine, bypassing the lower part of the stomach and part of the small intestine. After gastric bypass surgery, a patient can only tolerate small amounts of food due to the reduced size of their stomach. Patients usually lose a substantial amount of weight. Gastric bypass surgery does carry risks: damage to the spleen, pneumonia, vitamin deficiencies, anemia, and ulcers. But since it is often a last resort for extremely obese people, most feel the risks are worthwhile.

Adults are not the only ones who undergo surgery for weight loss. Many severely obese adolescents have bariatric surgery even though it is risky. The possible complications include internal bleeding, blood clots, and infections. Many doctors will not perform stomach surgery on teenagers because of the possibility of stunting their growth. Some teens who have had bariatric surgery might never reach their full height.

Doctors who do perform this surgery on teens have strict criteria: patients must have been unable to lose weight after six months in an organized weight loss program; they should be mature enough to stick to strict dietary guidelines after surgery; and they must be severely obese and suffering from obesity-related health problems. The teen must also receive counseling and support after the surgery.

Many options are available to individuals who want to lose weight. Yet, the obesity rate increases every year. James O. Hill, a physiologist at the University of Colorado's medical center, told the Associated Press, "If obesity is left unchecked, almost all Americans will be overweight by 2050."[2]

This woman battles a compulsive eating disorder.

*Wrestling coach Gary Jonseck lost nearly 200 pounds (91 kg)
after having gastric bypass surgery.*

RESPONSIBILITY

In December of 2001, the U.S. Surgeon
General issued a call to action concerning
obesity. Health and Human Services Secretary,
Tommy G. Thompson, stated:

Overweight and obesity are among the most pressing new health challenges we face today. Our modern environment has allowed these conditions to increase at alarming rates and become a growing health problem for our nation. By confronting these conditions, we have tremendous opportunities to prevent the unnecessary disease and disability they portend for our future.[1]

The call to action included suggestions such as changing the focus of obesity from one of appearance to one of health. It suggested educating health care providers about preventing and treating obesity as well as educating students about balancing a good diet with physical activity. It recommended more facilities for physical activity in schools, workplaces, and communities. The call to action recommended adopting policies that limit unhealthy foods in schools as well as increasing research into the causes and treatment of obesity.

The report described the cost of obesity in the United States. In the year 2000, the total cost of obesity amounted to $117 billion. These costs included health care, health insurance premiums, and lost work time. Conditions such as asthma, diabetes, cancer, and heart disease had also increased. This led to higher costs for taxpayers who fund government medical programs, as well as workers who contribute to company health insurance plans.

The report included a quote from Surgeon General David Satcher, who said, "People tend to think of overweight and obesity as strictly a personal matter, but there is much that communities can and should do to address these problems."[2] Is it the responsibility of communities and government to fight obesity? Or is it a personal responsibility? This is an argument that continues to rage.

Keep the Government Out of Our Kitchens and Restaurants

Many people firmly believe that the government has no business interfering in what we eat. Critics do not want the government to create laws and initiatives to ban snacks and sodas from school, outlaw trans-fats in restaurants, and impose fat taxes on unhealthy foods. Instead, they believe the government should create a feeling of personal responsibility in its citizens and urge them to make positive choices for their health and well-being. Opponents to government programs want to allow health insurers to charge lower premiums for healthy people. This would give people a financial incentive for staying fit and healthy. As Radley Balko stated in the *Time* magazine article "Are You Responsible for Your Own Weight?":

> *Give Americans moral, financial, and personal responsibility for their own health and obesity is no longer a public matter but a private one—with all the costs, concerns and worries of being overweight borne only by those people who are actually overweight.*[3]

LET GOVERNMENT CONTROL OUR DIET

Supporters of government intervention believe that the food industry should claim more responsibility for the rising rates of obesity. Food companies market unhealthy foods to consumers, who then buy unhealthy foods. Food companies claim that they only respond to consumer demand. Yet

Ronald McDonald, Health Ambassador?

In 2005, the McDonald's restaurant chain made an effort to promote healthier eating and add more nutritious items to their menu. They also launched a campaign to send their icon, Ronald McDonald, into schools to promote healthy lifestyles. Because he is so widely recognized by children, he seemed to be a good choice for promoting a lifestyle that included proper eating and exercise. While many experts complained about his presence in schools, the American Academy of Pediatrics felt that it was a good start. They stated that the program could "take advantage of the fact that Ronald McDonald has such recognition with kids that if he tells them to get moving, maybe they will do it."[4]

they continue to advertise and promote unhealthy foods such as soft drinks, fast food, and sugary cereals, especially to children. Those who advocate more government regulation feel that the only way to reverse the obesity trend is to control what the food and restaurant industries can sell. As authors Kelly Brownell and Marion Nestle state in *Time*:

> *Governments collude with industry when they shift attention from conditions promoting poor diets to the individuals who consume them. Government should be doing everything it can to create conditions that lead to healthy eating, support parents in raising healthy children and*

Homeland Obesity

Some critics of the government's efforts to control the obesity epidemic have suggested that perhaps the United States needs a Department of Homeland Obesity. The department would focus on the obesity problem with the same degree of effort that the Department of Homeland Security did after the September 2001 terrorist attacks. This department would oversee and be responsible for all the different aspects of obesity, which are presently spread between several federal agencies. Currently, the National Institute of Health focuses on research. The Centers for Disease Control and Prevention handles prevention, and the U.S. Department of Agriculture is in charge of nutrition education in schools. A single agency could coordinate all these efforts.

Some states are creating policies on school nutrition that are more strict than the federal government's policies. Currently, 18 states regulate school nutrition at a higher level than the U.S. Department of Agriculture. Eleven state legislatures have considered either banning soft drinks and junk food or increasing sales tax on those items. Others are considering reinstating broader physical education requirements.

make decisions in the interests of public health rather than private profits.[5]

Americans cherish their freedom, including the freedom to eat what they want. However, some are beginning to blame fast food companies when their personal choices result in obesity and related health problems.

No Easy Answers

There is no perfect solution for combating obesity, despite the two sides of the argument that pit personal responsibility against government intervention. Perhaps the only answer to the debate lies in a combination of these two approaches, using both personal responsibility and government intervention. As the Surgeon General said in his call to action, "Individuals, families, communities, schools, worksites, health care, media, industry, organizations, and government must determine their roles and take action to prevent and decrease overweight and obesity."[6]

Paying for Obesity

Just how much does it cost to be overweight? A study found that every year, in comparison to a person of average weight, the amount paid by the average overweight person for medical care increased by $247. For an obese person it increased by $732. These increasing costs are one of the biggest arguments used by people who do not feel that healthy taxpayers and health insurance participants should have to pay for the medical costs of the obese who share the same medical coverage.

The answer to obesity does lie in personal responsibility: a responsibility not only for our own diet and physical activity, but also responsibility as voters to decide how much government regulation should exist in order to reduce obesity. As Eric Schlosser states in his book *Chew on This*, it all comes down to personal choice:

> *The food you eat enters your body and literally becomes part of you. It helps determine whether you'll be short or tall, weak or strong, thin or fat. It helps determine whether you will enjoy a long, healthy life or die young.*[7]

Everyone must make their own choices, either in their personal lifestyle or in how they use their voting power as citizens to tell their government officials exactly how much they want legislation to be a part of the nation's menu. ⌐

Health Literacy

In his speech before the U.S. House of Representatives in 2003, Surgeon General Richard Carmona spoke about health literacy as the ultimate weapon against obesity: "Health literacy is the ability of an individual to access, understand, and use health-related information and services to make appropriate health decisions. ... As Surgeon General, I charge you to make healthy personal choices in your own lives, and to set good examples for all the children around you. And I ask you to work with me to support our efforts to improve Americans' health literacy, to put prevention first, and to end our nation's obesity epidemic before it has a chance to reach into another generation of Americans."[8]

Personal responsibility is an important part of the debate over obesity and its legislation.

TIMELINE

1916	1924	1935
The first national nutritional guide is developed by the Department of Agriculture.	American biologist Clarence Birdseye develops a process for quick-freezing foods, making Americans less dependent on fresh, seasonal food.	Cornell University researchers discover that rats eating nutritional meals live longer than those that eat what they want.

1968	1971	1994
Life magazine exposes the dangers of amphetamine diet pills.	Japanese researchers discover high-fructose corn syrup.	Researchers discover the hormone leptin, which plays a role in appetite.

1940	1950	1960
The microwave oven is invented and consumers can prepare meals in minutes.	The newest weight-loss fad at Slenderella Salons is the use of vibrating tables and diets.	The first diet food, Metrecal, is introduced. Overeaters Anonymous is started.

1996	1997	1998
The synthetic fat olestra is approved by the FDA and is a popular "low fat" additive to foods because it is not absorbed in the intestines.	The FDA issues a warning about the diet drugs fenfluramine and dexfenfluramine.	The National Institute of Health declares that 97 million Americans are overweight or obese.

TIMELINE

2000	2001	2002
The overall national costs related to obesity reach $117 billion.	The Surgeon General reports that 61 percent of Americans are overweight.	Three New Yorkers sue fast-food restaurants, claiming the fast-food companies are responsible for their obesity.

2004	2005	2006
Morgan Spurlock eats McDonald's food for 30 days and produces a documentary, *Supersize Me.*	The U.S. Department of Agriculture revises its food pyramid guide.	Eric Schlosser publishes *Chew on This*, an exposé of the fast-food industry written for young readers.

2002

McDonald's and snack food company Frito-Lay announce that they will remove trans fats from their foods.

2003

The lawsuits against the fast-food restaurants are dismissed.

2003

Surgeon General Richard Carmona announces that obesity has become a health crisis.

2006

Former President Bill Clinton and Governor Mike Huckabee persuade Coca-Cola and Pepsi to remove soft drinks from schools by the year 2010.

2006

Disney ends its agreement with McDonald's to provide toys for Happy Meals.

2007

Trans fats are banned from restaurants and bakeries in New York City.

ESSENTIAL FACTS

AT ISSUE

The debate over obesity centers on who is responsible for dealing with the crisis. Is the government responsible for legislating our diets and food choices, or is it the responsibility of the individual to maintain a healthy weight? Some people feel it is a loss of personal freedom if the government makes choices on their behalf as to what they can eat. But others point out that on a personal level, obesity rates continue to rise, and people are not doing enough to manage their weight.

In Favor:

❖ The obesity issue should be addressed through government actions that eliminate vending machines in schools, revamp school lunch and physical fitness programs, and educate people about proper nutrition and exercise.

❖ Some states and cities have begun to outlaw unhealthy ingredients such as trans fats from restaurants in their areas.

❖ If the government does not regulate food choices, the additional health care costs related to overweight and obesity affect everyone.

Opposed:

❖ Individuals are the only ones who ultimately decide what to eat and when to exercise.

❖ Various diets and diet support groups are flourishing, as are prescription diet pills and surgery.

❖ If an individual weighs more, he or she should be responsible for paying the difference in health care costs.

CRITICAL DATES

1972
Americans spent $3 billion on fast food.

1991–1999
The percentage of high school students taking physical education classes dropped from 42 percent to 29 percent.

1999
Approximately 61 percent of adults, 13 percent of children, and 14 percent of adolescents were overweight or obese. This is nearly triple the rate of 20 years ago.

2003
Americans spent $110 billion on fast food.

QUOTES

"Completely missing from the new [diet book] genre was one increasingly strange and distant concept: self-control. No, it was all a matter of using nutritional science to "trick" the body into doing what it should be doing anyway."—*author Greg Critzer*

"Governments collude with industry when they shift attention from conditions promoting poor diets to the individuals who consume them. Government should be doing everything it can to create conditions that lead to healthy eating, support parents in raising healthy children and make decisions in the interests of public health rather than private profits."—*authors Kelly Brownell and Marion Nestle*

ADDITIONAL RESOURCES

SELECT BIBLIOGRAPHY

Critser, Greg. *Fat Land: How Americans Became the Fattest People in the World*. Boston: Houghton Mifflin, 2004.

Ingram, Scott. *Want Fries with That? Obesity and the Supersizing of America*. New York: Franklin Watts, 2005.

Schlosser, Eric. *Fast Food Nation*. Boston: Houghton Mifflin, 2001.

Schlosser, Eric, and Charles Wilson. *Chew on This: Everything You Don't Want to Know About Fast Food*. Boston: Houghton Mifflin, 2006.

FURTHER READING

Abramovitz, Melissa. *Diseases and Disorders: Obesity*. Farmington Hills, MI: Lucent Books, 2004.

Collins, Tracy Brown, ed. *At Issue: Fast Food*. Farmington Hills, MI: Greenhaven Press, 2005.

WEB LINKS

To learn more about obesity and food policing, visit ABDO Publishing Company on the World Wide Web at **www.abdopublishing.com**. Web sites about obesity and food policing are featured on our Book Links page. These links are routinely monitored and updated to provide the most current information available.

For More Information

For more information on this subject, contact or visit the following organizations.

National Association to Advance Fat Acceptance (NAAFA)
P.O. Box 188620, Sacramento, CA 95818
916-558-6880
www.naafa.org/
NAAFA is a national nonprofit organization that seeks to improve the quality of life for overweight and obese people. This association attempts to eliminate size discrimination and offers tools for self-acceptance.

Partnership for Healthy Weight Management
www.consumer.gov/weightloss/index.htm
This coalition of representatives from the science, academia, and health-care fields, and government and commercial organizations promotes strategies for achieving and maintaining healthy weight loss.

Society for Nutrition Education (SNE)
7150 Winton Drive, Suite 300, Indianapolis, IN 46268
317-328-4627 or 800-235-6690
www.sne.org/
SNE represents professional nutrition educators by educating and influencing policy makers about nutrition, food, and health.

GLOSSARY

amphetamine
A drug that stimulates the central nervous system and is used to control appetite or depression.

bariatric surgery
Surgery on the stomach or intestines to control morbid obesity.

barrage
A concentrated outpouring, usually of questions or information.

blood pressure
The amount of force needed to pump blood to and from the heart.

caliper
A measuring device often used to measure body fat thickness.

carbohydrate
A basic component of food that provides energy to the body; a carbohydrate can be either complex or simple.

discrimination
Treating people differently based on their characteristics or group, rather than personal merit.

epidemic
A disease affecting many people at once and spreading across the population.

gastrointestinal
Relating to the stomach and intestines.

gene
The part of a DNA (deoxyribonucleic acid) molecule that passes hereditary traits from parents to their children.

glucose
A simple sugar produced in plants and animals when the body converts carbohydrates and proteins into energy.

hypothyroidism
> A condition where the thyroid does not produce enough thyroid hormone to properly regulate weight.

insulin
> A hormone that allows cells to absorb glucose or sugar.

leptin
> A recently discovered hormone that helps regulate appetite.

metabolism
> The process the body uses to break down food and send it to cells through the bloodstream.

morbid obesity
> A condition where a person is so obese that they are likely to have severe medical problems.

osteoarthritis
> A disease where the joints and cartilage of the body break down, often associated with obesity.

sedentary
> Getting very little physical exercise and spending most of the time sitting or not moving.

trans fat
> An artificial man-made fat that increases the fatty plaque in the blood and hardens the arteries.

triglyceride
> A type of fat found in the bloodstream.

SOURCE NOTES

Chapter 1. An Obesity Epidemic?

1. Richard H. Carmona. "The Obesity Crisis in America." Speech. 16 July 2003. U.S. House of Representatives. <http://www.surgeongeneral.gov/news/testimony/obesity07162003.htm>.

2. "Obesity and overweight." World Health Organization. 2007. <http://www.who.int/dietphysicalactivity/publications/facts/obesity/en/print.html>.

3. Greg Critser. *Fat Land: How Americans Became the Fattest People in the World*. Boston: Houghton Mifflin, 2004. 32.

4. "Obesity and Overweight." World Health Organization. 2007. <http://www.who.int/dietphysicalactivity/publications/facts/obesity/en/print.html>.

5. Kathleen Keller. E-mail to the editor. 27 Aug. 2007.

6. Richard H. Carmona. "The Time/ABC News Summit on Obesity." June 2004. *Time*. <http://www.time.com/time/2004/obesity/>.

Chapter 2. What Is Obesity?

1. "What Is Obesity?" American Obesity Association Fact Sheet. 20029* <http://www.obesityusa.org/subs/fastfacts/obesity_what2.shtml>.

Chapter 3. The Era of Supersizing

1. Quoted in *The Associated Press*, "Monster Thickburger Met with Mixed Reaction," 6 Dec. 2004. http://www.msnbc.com/id/6661977

2. Ibid.

3. Eric Schlosser and Charles Wilson. *Chew on This: Everything You Don't Want to Know About Fast Food*. Boston, MA: Houghton Mifflin, 2006. n.p.

4. "Man Blames 4 Fast Food Chains for His Obesity." 27 July 2002. *The Milwaukee Journal Sentinel*. Find Articles. <http://findarticles.com/p/articles/mi_qn4196/is_20020727/ai_n10815842>.

5. Eric Schlosser. *Fast Food Nation: The Dark Side of the All-American Meal*. Boston, MA: Houghton Mifflin, 2004. n.p.

6. Legal brief, "NY Dismisses First Fast Food Lawsuit." <http://biotech.law.lsu.edu/cases/food/Pelman_v_McDonalds_SDNY_brief.htm>.

Chapter 4. Teaching Obesity

1. Gordon W. Gunderson. "The National School Lunch Program Background and Development." U.S. Department of Agriculture Food and Nutrition Service. <http://www.fns.usda.gov/cnd/Lunch/AboutLunch/ProgramHistory_5.htm>.
2. Karen Springen. "School Lunch Daze." 2 Nov. 2005. *Newsweek*, <http://www.msnbc.msn.com/id/9889903/site/newsweek/>.
3. "School Lunch Program: Efforts Needed to Improve Nutrition and Encourage Healthy Eating." United States General Accounting Office Report to Congressional Requesters. 19–20. May 2003. <http://www.gao.gov/news.items/d03506.pdf>.
4. Ted Villaire. "The Decline of Physical Activity: Why Are So Many Kids Out of Shape?" Parent Teacher Association. <http://www.pta.org/archive_article_details_1118167427046.html>.

Chapter 5. Obesity and Health

1. "New State Data Show Obesity and Diabetes Still On the Rise." 31 Dec. 2002. 14 Nov. 2007 <http://www.cdc.gov/od/oc/media/pressrel/r021231.htm>.
2. "A Global Threat." *AICR Science Now*. Winter 2003. American Institute for Cancer Research. <http://www.aicr.org/site/News2?abbr=res_&page=NewsArticle&id=7440>.

Chapter 6. Obesity and Mental Health

1. Judy Battle. "It Hurts to Be Me." 2004. *Overweight Teen*. 14 Nov. 2007 <http://www.overweightteen.com/hurtstobeme.html>.
2. "The Psychological Consequences of Obesity in Children and Teens." *Overweight Teen*. <http://www.overweightteen.com/psychological.html>.
3. Story #13, "My Story," American Obesity Association. 2 May 2005. 14 Nov. 2007 <http://obesity1.tempdomainname.com/subs/story/entirestory.shtml>.
4. Ibid.
5. "Discrimination." American Obesity Association, 2002. <http://obesity1.tempdomainname.com/discrimination/employment.shtml>.

Source Notes Continued

6. Story #13, "My Story," American Obesity Association. 2 May 2005. 14 Nov. 2007 <http://obesity1.tempdomainname.com/subs/story/entirestory.shtml>.

Chapter 7. Legislating Our Diets
1. "Prevalence of Overweight and Obesity Among Adults: United States, 1999–2002." Jan. 2007. National Center for Health Statistics. Center for Disease Control. <http://www.cdc.gov/nchs/products/pubs/pubd/hestats/obese/obse99.htm>.
2. "Vending Machines in Schools," National Conference of State Legislatures. 1 Mar. 2005. 14 Nov. 2007 <http://www.ncsl.org/programs/health/vending.htm>.
3. Nanci Hellmich and Bruce Horovitz. "NYC Proposes Ban on Trans Fats in Restaurant Food." 26 Sep. 2006. *USA Today*. <http://www.usatoday.com/news/health/2006-09-26-nyc-cooking_x.htm>.
4. Tracy Jan. "N.H. Weighs Students to Monitor for Obesity." 30 Dec. 2004. *Boston Globe*. <http://www.boston.com/news/local/articles/2004/12/30/nh_weighs_students_to_monitor_for_obesity>.
5. Ibid.
6. Childhood Obesity. "Schools," American Obesity Association. 2 May 2005. 14 Nov. 2007 <http://obesity1.tempdomainname.com/subs/childhood/prevention.shtml>.

Chapter 8. Making Our Own Changes
1. Greg Critser. *Fat Land: How Americans Became the Fattest People in the World*. Boston, MA: Houghton Mifflin, 2004. 53.
2. Ibid. 3.

Chapter 9. Responsibility
1. "Overweight and Obesity Threaten U.S. Health Gains." 13 Dec. 2001. U.S. Department of Health and Human services. <http://www.surgeongeneral.gov/news/pressreleases/pr_obesity.htm>.
2. Ibid.
3. Radley Balko, Kelly Brownell, and Marion Nestle. "Are You Responsible for Your Own Weight?" 7 June 2004. *Time*. <http://www.time.com/time/magazine/article/0,9171,994398,00.html>.

4. Caroline E. Mayer. "McDonald's Makes Ronald a Health Ambassador." *Washington Post*. 28 Jan. 2005. 14 Nov. 2007 <http://www.washingtonpost.com/wp–dyn/articles/A43011–2005Jan27.html>.

5. Radley Balko, Kelly Brownell, and Marion Nestle. "Are Your Responsible for Your Own Weight?" 7 June 2004. *Time*. <http://www.time.com/time/magazine/article/0,9171,994398,00.html>.

6. "Overweight and Obesity: A Vision for the Future." 11 Jan. 2007. United States Department of Health and Human Services. <http://www.surgeongeneral.gov/topics/obesity/calltoaction/fact_vision.htm>.

7. Eric Schlosser and Charles Wilson. *Chew on This: Everything You Don't Want to Know About Fast Food*. Boston, MA: Houghton Mifflin, 2006. 9.

8. Richard H. Carmona. Testimony before the Subcommittee on Education Reform. 16 Jul. 2003.

INDEX

ABOUT THE AUTHOR

Marcia Amidon Lusted has written ten nonfiction books for children, as well as many magazine articles. She is also a writing instructor and a musician. She lives in New Hampshire with her husband and three sons.

PHOTO CREDITS